Backwater Musings

Poems from Virginia's Eastern Shore

by

Kendall Bradley

Copyright © 2020 by Kendall Bradley

All rights reserved.

ISBN 978-1-62806-287-8 (print | paperback)

Library of Congress Control Number 2020913757

Published by Salt Water Media
29 Broad Street, Suite 104
Berlin, MD 21811
www.saltwatermedia.com

Cover image and author photo courtesy of the author

for Ronda
my Shore girl,
my true love, my muse

In memoriam
Bobby Swain
Mary Ann and Milford Bradley

Previous publication credits:

Backwater Moon: "From Onley Looking South," "American Bittern," "Day-break," "My Grandmother," "Little Oyster Bay," Three Fragments of the Moon at Burton's Bay," "After Chopping Firewood in November," "Cat's Hammock," "November 2003," "Onley, Virginia December 8, 1973 (At the Verge of the Energy Crisis)," "On the East Side of Chincoteague," "When Marijuana Is Disguised As Winstons, Kools, Or Lucky Stripe Filters, There Is Little School Authorities Can Do," "The Witches of Hacks Neck," "Wachapreague," "Watermen," "Sixth Grade Transfer Student at Exmore-Willis Wharf School," "Autumn," "Nickawampus," "Thoughts of Wood," "A Visit," "Black Narrows," "Snow," "Backwater," "I Wonder What Sunsets Look Like In Istanbul," "I Knew You Before I Even Met You," "In Quinby," "My Bones," "The Cabin," "The Heart Knows," "Plato," "Glimpses," "Cold Rain."

A Butterfly with Teeth: "Upper Bayside, Accomack County," "Piano Jack," "Seaside Road," "Stepping Out for Some Fresh Air," "Evening," "Land of In-Between," "Available Delights," "Oyster, VA (Three Poems)," "Fire Lovers," "Listening," "The Marsh at Dusk (For the Children)," "Morris," "Percy's Closet," "Even for This," "La Mer," "The Foxes of Quinby," "Lightning Bugs."

Vicinity of Time: "Poem to Myself," "Having Survived Another Day of Teaching School I Wonder What I Am Going to Do with My Life," "Ghosts," "Near an Archaeological Dig Somewhere on the Seaside," "Eastern Shore," "Winter Storm," "Regarding a Recent Headline."

At the Edge of Mercy: "Seaside," "A Moment of Insight and Clarity," "Railroad Towns," "Box Tree Road Tryst," "Abandoned House in Moonlight," "Thinking Back 60 Years, Remembering Sam," "On the Porch," "Rancor," "Return," "Mortality," "On the Deck," "Bicycle Chronicles," "When All Has Been Taken From Me."

*Come, let me show you this, my native land,
This strippling that divides the bay and sea,
And grips with grim tenacity of saltbush
root and grass, to hold its own...*

−Katherine Roberts Wescott

*It is our inward journey that leads us through time −
forward or back, seldom in a straight line,
most often spiraling. Each of us is moving,
changing, with respect to others. As we discover,
we remember; remembering, we discover;
and most intensely do we experience this
when our separate journeys converge.*

−Eudora Welty

Table of Contents

Introduction 1

From Onley Looking South 2

Seaside 3

A Moment of Insight and Clarity 4

Ghosts 5

Box Tree Road Tryst 6

American Bittern 7

Abandoned House in Moonlight 9

Thinking Back 60 Years, Remembering Sam 10

On the Porch 12

Rancor 13

Return 14

Mortality 15

On the Deck 16

Upper Bayside, Accomack County 18

Day-break 19

Daddy Wise 20

My Grandmother 21

Piano Jack 23

Seaside Road 24

Stepping Out for Some Fresh Air 26

Evening 27

Land of In-Between 28

Glory Daze 29

Available Delights 30

Oyster, VA (Three Poems)	31
Fire Lovers	33
Listening	34
The Marsh at Dusk (For the Children)	35
Morris	36
Percy's Closet	37
Poem to Myself	38
Even for This	39
Having Survived Another Day of Teaching School, I Wonder What I Am Going to Do with My Life	40
Little Oyster Bay	41
Railroad Towns	42
Near an Archaeological Dig Somewhere on the Seaside	43
Eastern Shore	44
Winter Storm	47
La Mer	49
The Foxes of Quinby	50
Three Fragments of the Moon at Burton's Bay	52
Regarding a Recent Headline	53
After Chopping Firewood in November	54
Cat's Hammock	55
November 2003	56
Onley, Virginia December 8, 1973 (At the Verge of the Energy Crisis)	57
On the East Side of Chincoteague	58
When Marijuana Is Disguised As Winstons, Kools, Or Lucky Stripe Filters, There Is Little School Authorities Can Do	59

Bicycle Chronicles	60
The Witches of Hacks Neck	62
Wachapreague	64
Guard Shore	65
Watermen	66
Sixth Grade Transfer Student at Exmore-Willis Wharf School	67
Autumn	68
Nickawampus	69
Thoughts of Wood	73
Lightning Bugs	74
Forgotten	76
A Visit	77
Black Narrows	81
Snow	82
Backwater	83
I Wonder What Sunsets Look Like In Istanbul	85
I Knew You Before I Even Met You	87
In Quinby	89
My Bones	90
The Cabin	91
The Heart Knows	93
Plato	94
Glimpses	95
When All Has Been Take from Me	96
Cold Rain	97

Introduction

The Eastern Shore of Virginia lies at the southern tip of the Delmarva Peninsula, a narrow finger of land extending southward between the Atlantic Ocean and the Chesapeake Bay. Since the early sixteen hundreds, the Shore has been a backwater of Virginia, sometimes even inadvertently left off maps of the Commonwealth. Its geographic isolation (it was not physically connected to the rest of the state until the Chesapeake Bay Bridge-Tunnel was opened in 1964) has contributed to its uniqueness and slower pace of life. It is a land of hardy and pragmatic people, of tiny towns and sleepy villages, of fertile farmland, pine forests, and waterways teeming with seafood. It is an area rich in history and charmed with abundant natural beauty. Barrier islands fringe the Atlantic side separated from the mainland by winding creeks, broad bays, and vast stretches of salt marsh. Bayside creeks run from the spine of the peninsula into the storied Chesapeake, one of the largest estuaries in the world. Place names such as Chincoteague, Assawoman, Accomac, Onancock, Wachapreague, Nassawadox, Machipongo, and Kiptopeke hearken back to the area's original Algonquin inhabitants. Along the byways of the Shore, the economic extremes which have existed for centuries are apparent in ramshackle shanties and elegant historic homes. In isolated areas, abandoned houses dot a somber landscape presenting themselves in crepuscular light as mysterious and melancholy ghosts from days long past. In short, the Eastern Shore is a place where the raw material of poetry eloquently abounds.

The poems herein are a collection of the author's verse which spans a period of fifty years and, while there are a few new poems, most of them have been gleaned from books already published. The common thread of all of them is that they are somehow related, whether obliquely or directly, to this special place of which the author is a proud native.

Kendall Bradley
Melfa, Virginia
June 2020

From Onley Looking South

*The moon has forgotten us,
In darkness we wait*

Tonight, Debedeavon,
three hundred years
after your corpse lay
dry and bowless
in the holy tomb
of arched mats,
you are still alive.
I can hear your
haughty laughter
sweeping wind-like
from Kiptopeke
along forty miles
of rusty rail.

Tell me, then,
great "laughing King
of the Accawmackes,"
lord of thirty slender wives,
what have you to do
with the silent, whitewashed
towns of U.S. 13?
Do you forsake
the fierce orgies of the dead
to haunt this time and place?
Or do you come as an exile,
arrogant as a god
yet seeking birth
in a woman's womb?

Seaside

1
Here at the edge
of the continent,
at the borderland of
time and tide,
I discover
salt-gnarled cedars
and stunted pines
framing my view
to the east.

I find the mud-flat
hieroglyphics of heron tracks
and clam signs,
witness the ephemeral
dance of wind and light
over the broad bays,
catch the quick shadows
of sand sharks
in the shallows,
hear the osprey's
piercing cry before
its taloned plunge.

2
Beyond the reach
of upland swales
and marine railways,
out past the dark marshes
and oyster cultches,
beyond the shifting barrier islands
the white capped sea awaits.
Its distance-muffled roar
of transcendent indifference
seems to suggest a cadenced
and insistent prophecy
which yet remains
indecipherable and vague,
perhaps too strange
for human ears.

A Moment of Insight and Clarity

When he was
12 years old,
standing on a bridge
spanning a small
salt water gut
filled with minnows
at low tide,
he accidently blew off
part of his thumb
and index finger
with a silver salute.
No shock stunned
minnows floated
white bellied to
the surface that day
and it was a long
walk back home,
with the pain
throbbing like a
fish quivering
in the bottom
of a scow.

Ghosts

They gather
in moonlight
like wisps of memory
congregating
where back roads
stub out on the verge
of bayside guts.

They orgy
in their own
flickering way
among discarded
beer cans and used
condoms, fast food
wrappers and the gutted
carcasses of deer.

Their voices
are made of wind
and they take succor
however they may
as they move
into salt marsh or
pine woods

seeking untold things
in the crevices of night,
hurrying
to consummate
their secret deeds

before dawn's first
sunlight shimmer
of bejeweled
spartina.

Box Tree Road Tryst

Halfway to the creek
off Seaside Road,
black gum and salt pines
crowded the ditch banks
and this is where
we stopped the car.

It was late afternoon
on New Year's Eve
and Samba Pa Ti
was playing on the radio.

Recklessly, we got out
and danced slowly,
desperately,
defiantly,
on the cold tar and chip,
unexpectedly
putting on a show
for a lone waterman
on his way
to the landing.

So bittersweet it was
that we still talk about it

after all these years.

American Bittern

- for Bobby Swain

I.
As if sensing
its intrusive
discovery,
the sculpted
bittern stands
motionless as dusk,
bill upward
pointed as if
blending in
with reeds
around it,
uncanny
in its stark
beauty.

The bird
haunted the marsh
along the winding
creek where you
once lived
and worked.
A solitary creature
more often heard
than seen, it
was your first
and only bronze
casting.

It is my favorite
piece.

Tell me,
how did you feel
when you
first realized
you had captured cold
that sudden moment
of recognition
in such a simple

perfect flow
of indescribable
grace and
loneliness?

II.
I remember the day
we talked for a while
in your little shop
on Hunting Creek.
You told me you
would change nothing
about your life,
that you had long
ago made your peace
with the wheel chair
and now, more recently,
with the Parkinsons
which lay ahead.

These things
were your teachers,
you told me
in no uncertain
terms.

And even more –

life is what it is,
you seemed to say
without speaking
the words,

and we all pay
a price for
the little wisdom
we happen
to find.

We can be
grateful
or not.

It's up to us.

Abandoned House in Moonlight

In the ramshackle
rooms of the night,

the moon's bones
lie like broken glass
on warped floors
of aged heart pine.

The moon's face
is pinned upon a wall,
caught in a crooked smile
of cracked plaster.

And the lost children
of the moon are here,
shadows which seem
older than time.

They call out to me.

I listen as they
scuttle along
the baseboard
and vanish through
doorways of dream.

I feel them
beckoning to me

from the other side.

Thinking Back 60 Years, Remembering Sam

It would have
been best
not to look
into his eyes
at the moment
of sudden
realization,
right before
the first shot
rang out.

And best not
to look
as he fell
in an ungraceful
heap after
the second shot
finished him
off.

It would have
been best
not to watch
as they hooked
him and hung him
upside down
from the tripod
and slit
his throat
and his
steamy blood
ran out
into the big
porcelain pot.

It would have
been best
not to smell
the boiling hair
in the cast
iron kettle

or watch
the quick knives
do their work
on the butcher table
or see the dogs
fighting for pieces
of his heart
and lungs.

It would have
been best
just to eat
the sausage
and the bacon
and the ham
biscuits
later on
and not think
about our
former barnyard
buddy to whom
we felt so compelled
to give the name
of Sam.

On the Porch

Heat lightning
over the bay,
desultory ruminations
on a tottering porch,
a shadow creeps
along the creek bottom.

The past walks
home from the future
over the marsh,
bent and almost
unrecognizable,
its eyes glazed
with forbidden
knowledge.

What auguries are these?

My thoughts are
but vague ambiguities
blurred around the edges
like cedar tumps
in the sea mist.

Must I
Rorschach the clouds?
Read the entrails
of bewildering dreams?
Chart the osprey's
swoops and dives?

I close my eyes
and listen
to the rising wind.

Rancor

Exhausted by
the scrum of life
and feeling
homicidal,
I want to slit
rancor's vile throat
with a well-honed
oyster knife,
let it bleed out
beneath the moon
on the cold ground,
let it rot in place
all the winter long
to fertilize
spring dandelions

or better yet,
drag it down
to the marsh
on a flood tide,
weight it down
with ballast stones,
let its carbuncled
corpse be picked
clean by crabs
in the shallows.

Return

Memory curls
around these old trees
like wood smoke
that has no escape.

On the ground are
deciduous leaves,
deer droppings,
and thick shats
from loblollies
which muffle my steps.

I find the ditch,
now choked
with dead fall,
and the acrid smell
of stagnant water
closes in as I cross

to the small clearing
which was once
the beginning
of a field
that grew strawberries
and asparagus.

Soon, I stumble
on sheets of rusted tin,
remnants from the barn roof,
the rafters long since rotted
into the loam.

This means I am getting
close to where the house
once stood
and I see the spot,

a pile of rubble
obscured by honeysuckle
and closer to the barn
than I remember.

Mortality

The morning is
an albatross
forced from the sea,
bleeding from
its eyes.

Opaque forms
that seem to be people
move at the edge
of things,
beyond purpose
or intent.

A sullen wind arises.

Shadows
of shadows,
convex and concave,
dance in unison,
cry out,

lift their arms
toward me
as winged creatures
fly out of their
stubbed fingers

and stream inside me
to a place
that could be my heart.

They are brazen,
and I am afraid
they will eat me
alive, from
the inside out.

I feel them begin,
first a slight shudder,
then the gnawing
pain.

On the Deck

Finally we are
here together
and it's time
for the annoying
and troublesome
thoughts that are
the detritus of
the day to dissipate,
and they do so
grudgingly among
the cloud swirl
and early stars
of a broad sky.

I contemplate
the dark leaves
of maples
and wild cherry
along the borders
of the yard
and think
perhaps it's a
simple matter
of setting boundaries
at the edge of
the things
that somehow
take us in the wrong
direction.

Not such an easy
task when it
comes down to it.

A human life
is such
a frail thing
and intentions
can be frailer
still.

As you pour me
another glass
of wine,
I watch our cat,
who doesn't need
forgiveness
or redemption,
chase a doomed
insect into the night

and out on
the highway,
truckers run through
their gears,
destinations known
only to themselves.

We share a very
close life, you and I,
and I try to push aside
the nagging thought
that we all must
die alone in the end.

Last night,
I dreamed of
being skinned
alive by a faceless
antagonist,
with you watching,
frozen in horror,
from an upstairs
window of my
childhood home,
destroyed by fire
nearly fifty years
ago.

Upper Bayside, Accomack County

Beyond the ditch banks
just into the woods,
daffodils rise up
through February brambles
beside the tumbled steps
of the time haunted
houses of Messongo
and Marsh Market.

Glassless windows
with broken mullions
look out on back roads
like the dark eyes
of chary backwater girls
that are stuck forever
in sepia photos
from the 1930s.

Soon honeysuckle, wisteria,
and the leaves of sweet gum
will obscure the weathered
clapboard and sagging roofs

as they fade away
into lush springtime
shadows.

Day-break

Springing from
their ships of cloud,
Vikings
a thousand years old
have raided the night.
Vestiges
of their quick
slaughter
bloody the sky-rip
and blaze the slow
broad fields
all the way
to sea.

Daddy Wise

- for Greg, Bill, Ben, and Mike

It was a local teenage
rite of passage and
our time had come.

His modest clapboard home
sat outside town in
a cluster of somber dwellings
and late that night
the porch light was off.
We pulled into
his driveway
and stumbled to
the side door
through the darkness
in nervous anticipation.

After gaining the prize
more easily than
we had feared,
we chased Daddy's
bootlegged hooch
with Pabst Blue Ribbon
and raced down
the winding back roads
in a '62 Impala
like wayward princes
of the night.

We were young, dumb,
and full of cum
and we howled at the moon,
pissed in the ditches
and puked out our guts
on cold tar and chip
for the shear hell of it,
nearly 10,000 miles from
Da Nang, Khe Sahn and
the Ho Chi Minh trail.

My Grandmother

- for Ann Forbes

First, it was the nagging
fear of getting lost
in a familiar place
or missing trails
when she rode out,
at seventy, still
a dashing figure
on a frisky horse.

Later, it was being unable
to find a familiar place.
Even the barn became
an alien land, wrapped
in a fog of uncertainty.
She took some refuge
in old memories until
the distant past became
blurred in an iridescence
of strangeness.

In the beginning,
it was so hard on her
and in the end
it was even harder on us,
seeing her rich life reduced
to a protracted,
unintelligible whisper.

At her funeral,
I found myself thinking
about my last visit
to the nursing home
and how, as I was beginning
to leave, I suddenly
saw her as she must once
have been, during the war,
a woman in her prime
selling strawberries
at the Onley auctions,
her auburn hair tousled,

her blouse and hands
stained with the red
sweetness of June,

her good looks always
bringing her berries
the best prices.

Piano Jack

My grandfather
told me about
Piano Jack

how as a young man
he could
work the ivories
like a demon,
making you
go crazy and wild

or set you to crying
with the sheer
magic of his soft
touches.

He told me
how he was good
enough
for Philly
or Baltimore
or anywhere

but he got
into the horses
and he got
into the craps
and his luck
ran out

so they
broke both his hands
so bad

he could
hardly even cull potatoes
or feel up the girls
behind the grader shed

after that.

Seaside Road

- for Dave Harris

On the fringe of the continent
in early March light,
I drive the snaking black road
beside fields of winter
rye and ancient groves
of sycamore, oak
and loblolly pine,
past long lost graves
of masters and slaves,
of potato farmers
and Algonquin braves,
past doublewides and
tottering shacks,
ante-bellum mansions
and turn-of-the-century
farm houses.

From Magotha to Oyster,
Boxtree to Goshen,
Red Bank to Willis Wharf,
I hear the maritime musings
of raw-boned watermen
riding upon the sea wind.

I see the magic seaside loam
stretching to the woods,
the prairie-like marsh beyond
and winding guts leading
to barrier islands
or the dancing blue
of Ramshorn Bay.

It is indeed a good thing,
a sacred wisdom
to save what we can
of this menaced land

and thinking thus,
I think of you,
now retired in Virginia Beach

yet here still,
a presence not
imagined but felt
as I drive along.

We had different professions
but they overlapped,
to my benefit,
taking me time and time again
along the vistas of Seaside Road,
and over swale and slough
to the secret places
few have seen.

I need to thank you
for the gift,
and all that you taught me
along the way
in word and deed
before and after
I even knew
it was happening.

Sorry I did not tell you,
until now.

Stepping Out For Some Fresh Air

Clear winter
night sky,
frost already
on the deck rails.

In the moonlight,
a feral cat
slips beneath the shed
at the edge
of the yard

as a semi runs
through its gears
out on Route 13.

In the sky,
among the glimmer
of Ursa Major
and Cassiopeia,
the blinking lights
of planes head
to Norfolk
from Boston
or New York,

shiny fuselages
filled with their
captive cargo
of tedium and
untold dreams.

Evening

Form is emptiness. Emptiness is form. - The Heart Sutra

Geese are on the wing
over the winter marsh.
They honk and are gone,
heading east.

Near the landing,
a boat motor starts
and then sputters off,
suddenly mute.

At the edge of
a narrow gut near
a small tump of cedars,
I stop the sound
of my own feet

and suddenly
need to know:

who is this
who now listens
so intently
to the silence
of snow?

Land of In-Between

Strung along the highway
like amber jewels
in a necklace for the night,
the lights of
the little clapboard towns
of the Eastern Shore
appear suddenly out
of the rural darkness
then pass quickly
back into the same
greedy blackness,
little more than
electromagnetic whispers
shunting through the windshields
of Jersey bound truckers
and tourists speeding south
toward the boardwalks
and honky-tonks
of Virginia Beach.

Glory Daze

- for Larry Galloway

It was a league of small
high schools in rural Virginia.
We were farmers' sons
and doctors' sons,
the sons of watermen,
and furniture salesmen,
the sons of carpenters,
bankers and petty thieves.

As America channeled
breathlessly into the 60's,
the decade of assassinations
and British rock, of burning cities
and numberless body bags
on far away tarmacs,
we spent our Friday nights
from early September
to Thanksgiving
pounding on and crashing
against each other's bodies
like it was do or die,
like it was the be all
and end all of everything,

only to realize later
that tackles and touchdowns
were but a transient
glory at best,
because the vast world
was out there
beyond the lights,
waiting patiently
for each of us
and it was hungry
and mean
and so very
unimpressed.

Available Delights

Late May
or early June:
fresh picked asparagus
lightly sautéed
in butter,
fried seaside drum,
local strawberries
in simple syrup
topped with real
whipped cream...

I find myself
taking extra time
to savor fully
these precious
but fleeting
available delights

knowing they come
but once a year

and more years
might not come
at all.

Oyster, VA (Three Poems)

I.
Nine miles east of this tiny hamlet,
as the gull flies, the ocean batters
what is left of Cobb's Island,
inexorably pushing the narrow spit
westerly toward the mainland.

Northern millionaires
once embarked from Oyster slip
to dine on black duck
and sip expensive whiskey
on the veranda
of the island's renowned hotel
before its balustrades
became fancy driftwood
tossed into the marshes
by the great hurricane of 1896.

II.
Before the oysters gave out,
Herman "Hardtimes" Hunt lived
in a ramshackle house
outside of the village
and became its most famous son.

Philosopher, raconteur, rapscallion,
proprietor of the first and only Academy
of Clam Stomping and Oyster Shucking,
he once ran for the State Senate
and then Lieutenant Governor,
knowing full well that
life was too short
not to delight in its salty and
magical fresh shucked
sweetness.

III.
In a low hung cinder block building
hunkered down along the docks
near abandoned marine railways
and stacks of crab pots,
an unobtrusive salvation unfolds
as the sanguine future of oysters
moves restlessly in fiberglass vats.

The sterile tripoid spats greedily
feeding on plankton will soon be
on their way to floating upwellers
and then to cultches on the salty flats
of The Thorofare or Mockhorn Bay
where they will get fat and juicy
and ready for upscale
East Coast restaurants
and the seedy raw bars
of tourist towns.

Fire Lovers

Arson is almost as good as Prozac. -Joe Hill, The Fireman

The treacherous,
unforgiving,
moon dappled,
black shadowed,
twisting and sorrowful
midnight back roads
of Accomack County
call out to the
would be lovers:

ride me, ride me
without shame or regret
and show the world
your crazy unfulfilled love,
present the fragrance
of smoking wood
upon the alter
of love,
send the roaring orange
orgasmic flames
into the open arms
of the lonely night.

Do this
and the wild thrill
of your secret deeds
will be your
fiery passion
that will burn
and burn
and burn.

Note: Beginning in November 2012 in Accomack County, Virginia, a local volunteer fireman in league with his girlfriend went on a far flung arson spree which lasted five months and resulted in 86 fires of mostly abandoned buildings before they were caught. Reporting on this bizarre occurrence suggests that their troubled love life was enigmatically a major factor in their fiery deeds.

Listening

Racing
down the street
in front of our house,
two pocket rockets
splinter the night
into jagged pieces
and then speed on
to other roads.

I listen
as crickets and cicadas
and a nearby barn owl
slowly put the pieces
back together

and back yard
earth worms
return
to their dark
and silent
dreams.

The Marsh at Dusk (For the Children)

Beware the pompey
on the prowl
before the coming
of the night.

With seaweed hair
and bull shark teeth
he moves through
the marsh on silent
webbed feet.

His claws are
bleached bones
strong as steel
and his heart
throbs a bloody
tidal beat.

Taller than a man
and quicker than an eel,
he is coming for you.

His osprey eyes
can see tiny movements
far away
even in the dimming light

as he seeks
his evening meat.

Morris

*the voices said "do things, break things,
tear things, destroy things" - Morris Odell Mason*

Half man and half child,
he was the self-proclaimed
"killer for the Eastern Shore."

One night in 1978,
after two bottles of TJ Swann,
the demons called
and Morris answered.
He beat Miss Maggie
with an ax handle,
nailed her to
her living room chair
and burned
her house down.

From the shadows
he watched the flames
for a while before moving
down the railroad tracks
to another town
and other deeds.

Seven years later,
oblivious to the candlelight vigil
outside the penitentiary walls,
an unrepentant Morris requested
for his last meal two Big Macs
and a diet Coke.

Percy's Closet

Deep in the woods
off Bradford's Neck Road
the ghostly dresses
were lovingly hung
in the moonlight
on wires spread
from bough to bough,
and they would flutter
in the breeze
like gossamer dreams.

From this ethereal
wardrobe Percy chose
the cotton dresses
he wore to the Wachapreague
carnival each July,
where for one ticket he
could ride and ride and ride
on the merry-go-round,

beguiled by the music,
and the lights,
and the french-fries,

and the giggling,
gesturing children.

Poem to Myself

The two AM moon rises,
a fiery wreck
from some forgotten sea
as loblolly
and sweet gum
tear songs
from this westerly gale.
I stand barefoot
on the cold
kitchen floor,
fleeing dreams
to drink a glass
of cool water
from a deep well.

What a night
to walk in the woods
raising old bones
from their forgetful sleep!
What a night to die there
unheard and unseen,
an imperceptible shadow
motionless
among darker shadows
dancing...

Even For This

I.
In the slow motion
of forsaken time,
in darkness
and a forlorn wind,
a backwater creek
is being dragged for corpses,
the hard-eyed boatmen
are peering at
the search-lit water,
the onlookers are standing
at the edge of the marsh
like wounded herons
in the cold shadows.

II.
It is a cruel dawn
that offers no solace
from a merciless night
and a cruel day
that follows.

Yet,
we are made
even for this,

even for this.

Having Survived Another Day of Teaching School I Wonder What I Am Doing With My Life

It is dusk
and I sit on a stump
of seasoned oak
in front of the barn,
watching the day
fade slowly across
fields heavy with
spring.

In town,
nestled with precision
among stately Victorians
and squat ranchers,
the street lights
begin to flicker
their harmless defiance
at the coming night.

As I light my pipe,
an old sedan
explodes by,
the ugly staccato
of its torn muffler
rips through my veins
with the senseless
violence of sudden
acceleration.

When it is gone,
finally swallowed by a long
stretch of crushed stone,
the wind still ripples
the tall, slim-stemmed oats
in front of me, bending
incomprehensible
patterns toward
the darkened woods.

Little Oyster Bay

You read Bukowski
to me as I fixed
omelets on that first
Sunday morning.
It was a three month lease.
The house was smallish
but it had a large deck,
a chiminea, a dock,
and that view, my god,
that view...

It was late January
and the wind never
stopped blowing
and I remember moments
of bold, brash happiness
like I have never known
and I remember the tears,
so many tears
as we could not help
but cut ourselves
on our own sharp,
jagged edges.

We made love
morning and night
and I believed it to be
the best three months
of my life.

Guilt, remorse,
unspeakable joy –
the eternal conflict
of the human soul.

Yes, I remember the tears,
but I also remember
the moon rising
over the dark spine
of Assateague Island
sending to us a path
of dancing light
across Little Oyster Bay.

Railroad Towns

They sprang up
out of farmland
and woods when
the NY, P, & N
laid down the Virginia
track in 1884,
a straight bright
meridian of steel
from New Church
to Cape Charles
which created overnight
prosperity and
sudden wanderlust.

Ghosts of former
travelers to Wilmington
and Philadelphia crowded
the last passenger train
in 1958 on its short run
north to the Maryland line
but the romance
had long since died,
an accidental victim of
unrelenting progress.

Today the rusting rails
have been abandoned
even by the freight lines
and the old station depots
have disappeared or been
turned into storage sheds
or tiny museums.

The towns still stand
but most are smaller
and quieter now,
hunched along
the useless track
like aging jilted lovers
left unceremoniously
on the platforms,
watching their dreams
fade into the distance,
hoping for better days
that will never come.

Near An Archaeological Dig Somewhere on the Seaside

My spirit moves
through interstices,
peers into dark,
hollow places,
lifts the smooth
edges of dreams.

It soars through
cloud layers
of prehistoric bone
to dance
in solar wind.

Back to earth
it flies,
to forest and stream,
to dirt and stone.

It becomes an owl
perched on a black
limb in the dusk
and with owl eyes
watches as the night
moves in over
the marsh.

Eastern Shore

Pleistocene glacier spawn,
sea ooze, unconsolidated
silt and sand,
wind cast and storm swept
along the narrow
10,000 year old spine
stretched taught
between bay and sea,
dark streams flowing
east or west,
freshwater to salt,
winding creeks to tidal flats,
high marsh and low marsh
and oyster grounds,
barrier islands
on the Atlantic side
holding back the wild sea
yet moving, ever shifting
to the sea's command,
and on the bayside,
the wide creeks
leading to the deep
blue of the Chesapeake...

On the mainland
old growth forests of oak,
beech, black gum
and sycamore
now nearly gone,
loblolly pine
still sending tap roots deep,
seeking a way to thrive
near encroaching
salt marsh
and rising tides.
Gentle swale and undulation,
whale wallows,
broad fields of loamy sand
and sandy loam,
soils called Nimmo
and Polawana, Munden,
Bojac, and Molena,

potato and tomato land,
soy and barley
and spring wheat,
field corn which
dances beneath
autumn moons,
the bayside strawberry fields
long gone, the cropping
of yams and Haymans,
peas, onions, and squash,
mostly now
gray haired memories,

potstone and plough shards,
Algonquian flint
and musket balls,
mule skulls and bear jaws,
rusted shackles –
the earthy secrets
of the centuries
sometimes revealed,
blood and oaths
sometimes recalled,
the ghostly demarcations,
the King's patents,
the metes and bounds,
the stolen land
aggrandized,
bought and sold
but never possessed
by transits and rods
by macadam and asphalt
by tar and chip and concrete
by rail beds and power grids
by cul de sacs and billboards
by Walmart and Food Lion
by poultry houses
by combines and tractors
by crop dusters and four wheelers
by neon lights and traffic lights
by street lights and headlights...

for the land abides.

Ever waiting
between sea and bay,
the land abides,
ever dreaming
its *terra firma* dreams
the land abides,
beneath the stars
beneath the sun
beneath the moon

the land abides
while still it may.

Winter Storm

It is cold dark
and the old bones
of this house
moan in pain
as this winter nor'easter
has its fierce way,
showing no mercy
even to the ghosts
who will not
venture abroad tonight
but rather
have taken up their
tenuous habitation
inside my own skull
to ramble and sulk,
accuse, decry and defame
as they see fit.

The storm storms on
with ice, sleet, and snow
as we lie together,
warm in a heatless room,
twelve years to the night
we slept together
for the first time
choosing a new life,
becoming quiet,
tainted heroes
to ourselves and
anathema to those we hurt.

As the roiling sea
cuts new inlets
through the barrier islands,
destroys fishing piers
in tourist towns,
and sends salt water
darkly into the streets
of Wachapreague and
Chincoteague,

I think back those twelve years
to the sharp joy and
exquisite pain

of those days,
to our own storm of storms,
knowing that
if need be
I would
do it all again,
take the wild risk
again and again
over and over
forever,

and now wondering

had we not chosen
as we did,
had not chosen
the sweet hope of our love
over any consequence,

where would
I be now
and how well
would I be coping
with even the basic
simple things

such as a night-long
raging wind
or the inevitable
sun-bright calm
to follow?

La Mer

I would write
a eulogistic poem
about you
as so many
have done

but when I walk
beside you
on the moon strand
in the wind mist

I am overwhelmed
not by the romance
of your dark presence,
but by your vast otherness
and by what I fear
may be
your total lack
of intrinsic meaning.

Mother of all living
organisms on planet earth,
progenitor of
metaphor and myth,
how can this be?

In your presence,
I am muted
into uneasy silence.

I feel that I am
but a vagrant
on the dangerous shores
of your mercy,

making,
in spite of myself,
wordless supplication
to your
uncanniness

and to mine.

The Foxes of Quinby

The old heads
have never seen
anything like it.

They have been
showing up inexplicably
on front porches,
along the main street,
and under the culverts
at Bradford Acres.

Somebody said
coyotes have moved in
to Cat's Point
driving them out
of the woods.

No one knows for sure
but there are kittens
and toddlers to protect
and great grandmothers
who must walk to their sheds
for sundry things.

So the men take
target practice and
the trophy kills mount up,

but the foxes keep
coming,
out of the woods
out of the fields
into the yards
and driveways
in broad daylight.
They arrive
with an unexpected
nonchalance
and they are chased away
with shovels or shot
dead with a certain
exuberance.

Animal Control is no help
and the Game Commission
doesn't care
and the Health Department
is only interested in rabies.
Bring in the dead foxes
and we will saw
off their heads, they say,
and send them
for testing
to the Norfolk lab.

But rabies is not
really suspected,
as the foxes are not foaming
at the mouth or attacking
indiscriminately.
They are just showing up
at odd times and places
for no apparent reason.

So the trophy kills
mount up
as the foxes keep coming
with a kind
of relentless abandon
and their eyes
are as dark as
the night woods,
as dark as the marsh
with daylight faded,

as dark
as the wild blood
that drips down
the reddish fur
onto the ground
beside whitewashed
sheds in the Quinby
moonlight.

Three Fragments of the Moon at Burton's Bay

> *Cuando la luna entrega sus nauafragios,*
> *sus cajones, sus muertos*
> *- Neruda*

I.
Clever queen of shadows!
While you haunt the waves
between sea grass and Cedar Island,
forcing night into the marsh,
the birth and death
of your fulgent, leaping arcs
plunge another darkness
deep into the channel...

II.
Beneath a violent sky,
two watermen, wild with beer,
abandon their slick Chevies
and square off with oyster knives.
For a quarter hour
they flail and bleed
in the silence of sand,
thirty miles from the teasing
women of Pocomoke.

III.
Wind
and the absence of wind
are music.
I stand on this tottering dock
no longer afraid
that I have strayed too far
from the dance of dark,
deep-rooted pines.

Regarding A Recent Headline

Nor'easter,
sudden squall,
dead calm

the sea can kill.

Old salts know
the deep longing
of the sea

and its
ultimate indifference

once it's had
its way.

Last week,
another body
washed up
on the bayside
shore

and they are looking
for one more

and the sleek
craft, or pieces
thereof,

not so seaworthy
after all.

After Chopping Firewood in November

Cold and sharp
as the head of my ax,
the wind rushes at me
from the northwest.
If it were suddenly
to split me in two
with an invisible thrust,
part of me would sweep
up the jagged pieces
of pine and lunge
for the house,
while the rest of me,
hardly shivering in the chill,
would stay to watch
an orange moon
slip silently through
the bare, slim sumacs
on the other side
of the chicken pen.

Cat's Hammock

Old Alf said
there's a ghost
in this marsh,
said powerful
strange things
can happen here,
said he saw the moon
drown one night
right off this tump,
her cold brightness
dulled by a fathom
at flood tide.

Right thar,
she broke into pieces
tiny as aryster shells
and they spread with the toid
down Young Creek
yon to Jimmy's Gut
where they was taken
by crebs
in the shallers...

November 2003

I
Tonight,
from Swan's Gut Creek
to Kiptopeke,
the fire leaves
of autumn
have been cooled,
turned into
layers of gray
by the moon's
frosty breath.
Unable to sleep,
I stand outside
gazing up
at the impossible
vastness
of the Milky Way,
warmed simply
by the thought
of you.

II
The way you
look at me
I must wonder
what knowledge
you have conjured,
peering deep
into the backwaters
of my soul.
Perhaps you now
know me better
than I know myself.
But sometimes,
I fear you see there
the reflection
of your own dreams,
mistaking my dark
shallows
for deep water.

Onley, Virginia December 8, 1973
(At the Verge of the Energy Crisis)

Rain all day,
ice coming –
fear of a cruel winter
is widespread.
Already it is dark
and dogs,
crouched low
beneath houses,
shudder in the wind.

At the mayor's order,
the town still
sends its mercury
vapor street lights
in four directions
and now
near the laundromat
beneath one of those
lights, two laborers
in a '63 Chrysler
chug whiskey and beer.

Soon, they will
tear angrily
through the center
of town,
startling a few
citizens who lately,
in quiet, well lit rooms,
have been secretly
tortured by thoughts
of darkness.

On the East Side of Chincoteague

The wind
of shrieking wings
slashes from Assateague.
It tears wildly
at deep-rooted pines,
it rips the cruel
bodies of stray dogs,
it batters the cold,
black skeleton
of the Oyster Museum.

It quickens
a thin, red-eyed man
who stumbles
through the marsh
near the trailers,
screaming for his
daughter.

When Marijuana Is Disguised As Winstons, Kools, or Lucky Stripe Filters, There Is Little School Authorities Can Do (1975)

I.
Just outside the pale,
green doors,
some students from second lunch
lounge recklessly
against the cool,
red bricks of
the smoking area.

Here and there,
yellow-gray smoke
rises lazily up
the wall above them,
drifts briefly toward
the tall, chain-linked fence,
and melts
into open air.

II.
It is spring.

Across the drive
near the new vocational wing,
the dark leaves
of a single maple
bend gently in a breeze
that sings of
acres of dandelions
dropping slowly from
a midday crescent
moon.

Bicycle Chronicles

- for Milford

He was a solitary rider
and a man of few spoken
words.

The winding back roads,
which he knew better
than the veins
on the back of his own
sun-darkened hands,
were his private domain
and he put more miles
on two wheels than
many did on four.

His honesty and integrity
were legendary
and he would offer
his help to anyone
who had a need

but he was most alive
on the open road
when he could feel
the wind in his face
and be comfortable
in his own skin
and think his own
quiet thoughts

of sky and woods
of marsh and sea mist,
of little towns
and corn fields,
of October leaves
and ditch bank lilies.

I think he lived for
the smell of sudden rain
on hot tar and chip
and the friendly waves

from gardeners in
wide-brimmed hats
or from winos on tottering
front porches.

Yet we never talked
much about his rides
and all that he saw
from the seat of his
recumbent bike,

because we never talked much
about anything really.

This is why,
when my brother and I
cleaned out our parents'
house before putting
it up for sale,
I painstakingly searched,
though in vain,
for a fantasy of mine:
a diary, a memoir,
or just a sweat-stained
spiral notebook,

hoping against hope
to find secret
bicycle chronicles

written by my dad.

The Witches of Hacks Neck

From a long stand
of cedar and pine,
the three witches
of Hacks Neck,
two hunched women
and a stringy old man,
move over the marsh
at dusk
like pale owls,
their lanterns
extended before them
seeking the sudden gleam
of eels through
the high spartina.

At the sight of them,
dogs cower
with raised hair
beneath the docks,
and young children,
now recalling
admonitions made
only half in jest,
put their backs
to the marsh
and edge for home
a little early.

The three witches!
After all these years,
no one has befriended them,
preferring instead
to commit them
to tales with
a supernatural theme.

And why not?
ask the tired wives
of quick eyed watermen.
These three keep
always to themselves,
speaking only

in whispers like hoarse gulls.
They eat garbage and bait
fouled by the sun,

and when the bay storms,
turning leaves inside out
and driving small boats
to dock,

they stand at the door
of their hovel,
their eyes burning
with a strange,
flickering fire.

Wachapreague

A northwest wind dances
east from the Chesapeake
whirling through
fields of winter rye
and twelve miles
of ditches and power
line into the core
of this wooden town.
The tall frame houses
stand quietly in the dusk,
drawn into themselves
like cautious sentinels.

Out past the burned out
seventy year old hotel,
on the new marina,
the town's only wino
hunches for warmth
near a soda machine.
Beyond him,
the few boats at dock
sway to the end
of their ties and back,
hidden from the sea
by a dark maze of marsh
stretching all the way
to the sea-gnarled pines
of Parramore Island.

Guard Shore

It was just the two of us
with the winter beach
to ourselves,
drinking apple schnapps
and you reading to me
The Man with the Blue Guitar
and tears were streaming
down my face because
nobody ever read
Wallace Stevens to me
before and no woman ever
read poetry to me
except my mother
long, long ago.

And then we were out
of the car in the winter
cold. I reached for you
to pick you up but
my drunken knees
gave way. I hit the road first
and then you fell on top of me.
We could not stop laughing
and I kept holding you tighter
and tighter, would not
let you get up because
I didn't want the moment
to end and thinking: this,
this is what I have
been looking for these
ten thousand years
and I didn't even know it
until now.

Watermen

- for Ash, who died with his boots on

Wrinkled,
fog-kissed,
they left
the barnacled poles
at the break
of dawn.

One by one,
like delicate lovers,
they eased their scows
through the winding
dark marsh

and broke
into deep
water.

Sixth Grade Transfer Student at Exmore-Willis Wharf School

> *It is as though we all preferred*
> *to die to preserve our shadows.*
> *- R.D. Laing*

On the day you arrived,
the principal informed me
that your mother had placed
a revolver to her head
and blown out her brains
on Christmas Eve.
Tied in a chair, unwilling
to shut your eyes,
you witnessed the whole thing.

Later, I learned that she
was buried in cowboy clothes,
and the woman who stayed with you both
(the one who insisted that
you call your mother "dad")
had crumpled a twenty dollar bill
into one of the vest pockets
with a note saying: *maybe*
this will buy you a ticket to heaven.

After you left Florida
and came north to stay with an aunt,
this woman sent you pictures
of the open coffin
taken from every angle, in full color.
I remember the day you brought
the prints to school and asked me
if you could pass them around the class.
They were tucked neatly
in a large manila envelope
and, as you pulled them out
carefully in a single group,
you cautioned everyone to touch
only the clean, white borders.

Autumn

The wind gusts in
from the barrier islands,
running the tide up
high beyond the sedge
at Burton's Shore.
Inland six miles,
tall stalks of corn
bend and sway like
ancient dancers
while farmers in
battered combines
race relentlessly
against the thickness
of night.

The season of violence
has begun.

Already, the damp
grass is sharply cold
and dogs run wild
beneath the twisting
joints of trees.

Nickawampus

I
Algonquian stream
mill stream
backwater reach
to marshy creek...

He told me
that he came here
alone one night
in the winter of '47
drunk, bleeding
invisibly from his
secret wound,
his heart seeming
colder than
snow touch,
colder than
the sluggish stream
under ice.

For an hour
he walked beneath
the moon, listening
to a stranger
crunching snow
with footsteps
that seemed
nearly his own.

Restless
in the moonlight,
the geese
were bedding
in Kellam's field.
He crept near,
a shadow at the woods
edge, like a young
soldier once
in the Ardennes,
only this time
weeping, unable
to fire.

II
In the wet season
of 1977,
a crew of eight
on work release
with bush axes,
rakes, chain saw
and comealong,
are cleaning from
seaside mouth
to the old
Penn Central tracks
in Melfa
under the county
drainage program.

Today
at break time,
four miles from town,
they roll reefers
and butcher two
snappers by a lolly
stump fire.
The men joke
cars and women
and who knows
what.

Only one of them,
with hip boots
half rolled,
keeps to himself
along the bank,
notices deer tracks
at the swollen edge,
explores the coon
tracks further on
thinking this place
this place

as the leader signals
and the men stir
in slow motion
half warm and grumbling
back to work

and the chain saw,
greedy for wood flesh,
stutters, growls,
grinds its teeth
in the chill air,
its blue smoke
curling cedar green.

III
He watched
the osprey circle

again
high above,

the great wings
outstretched

answering
sudden eddies

with a single
undulation.

The girl lay
beside him

asleep on the bank.
Her eyes

at the trembling
moment

of love
were dark,

darker than the stream
where it joined

the winding creek.
And he feared

those eyes,
seeing something

of himself there
and now also

in the unyielding
blue

of the osprey's
sky.

Thoughts of Wood

As I grow older,
I like to think
my mind
is 19th century
heart pine,
clapboard on an old
barn that refuses
to topple,
weathering
to a glorified gray,
a distinctive grain,
unique and interesting,
with a twist of artsy
abstraction,
the passing courtesy
of sun, wind,
and storm.

But sometimes I fear,
it is more like
plywood,
with laminates
buckling from
too long
in the elements
of modernity,
acid rain and
recycled
East Coast smog,
the space age glue
inexorably dissolving,
the edges peeling
back toward
one another
in an unsettling
grin.

Lightning Bugs

Called fireflies
north of the Mason-Dixon line,
we tend to use
the more dramatic appellation
and we wait
from autumn to late spring
for the enchanting
cold fire ritual
of silent bioluminescent
mating calls
to begin anew.

I think of childhood summers
and the mason jars
with perforated lids
which made an almost
mystical sporadic light
in hot upstairs bedrooms
and how the bugs
would be dead by morning
if we didn't relent
and shake them
out the window
before drifting off to sleep.

I try not to think
of one summer night,
some years later,
as I sat nearly drunk
on the sagging front porch
of a house that no longer stands,
when the bugs were so thick
along the dark line of trees
at the wood's edge

that they seemed to me
like the dream time replay of
muzzle flash in a hot LZ

as once described to me
by a fellow collector
of lightning bugs

who didn't make it back
from his second tour
of Nam.

Forgotten

In forgotten places
like Belinda
and Winterville,
gaunt and empty houses
haunt the landscape
at the verge of
encroaching marsh.

Hunched for years
against bayside gales,
they now lean eastward,
their old bones
of weathered pine
spliced together
by honeysuckle vines
and bull briars.

They still have
stories to tell but
who will listen?

After dusk,
they sometimes
sing in the starlight
but only to themselves,
the doleful songs
of those whose
nights are lonely,
whose days are
numbered.

A Visit

- for Betty Bradley

I sat uneasily
in the neat
sitting room
of the old, converted
house, fixed
in the vacuous gaze
of four silent
patients.
Outside, the wind
tore at maple trees,
whipping paper
and dust across
the high school
athletic field.
Soon, the nurse
entered, smelling
of disinfectant,
and told me
you were in the ward
waiting for your
treatment.
Go on in, she said,
there is time.

The room was long
and narrow
with beds lining
both institution green
walls. You were
lying on your side
in an outside bed,
legs drawn up
fetus-like, gazing
down the row
of empty beds
ahead of you.

Gaunt, light
as a child,
yellow purple-veined

skin clinging
tightly to brittle bones,
you looked up
at me, said
I had grown heavier
and taller
in a year.
I managed a smile
and gave you
the basket
you had wanted,
the one I found
in your living room
filled with literature
from Oral Roberts
advertising precious
vials of healing oil
and trips
to the Holy Land.
Now, in early spring,
you were going to
use it to pot
a flower.

As usual, I
spoke few words,
not knowing what
to say.
There was no
awkward silence,
only awkward noise
as a lady
with angry red
doll eyes
propped in a bed
nearby began
to babble
constantly in loud
abusive tones
to a multitude of
phantoms.

You had grown used
to her, you said.
I didn't think so,

but who was I
to wonder?

I was never
close to you,
hardly even knew
you even after
all those years
of family dinners
every other
Sunday afternoon.
You were the best
cook, but our worlds
seemed always
tangential, they never
seemed to mesh.

Now, as you lay there
so helpless,
so alone, waiting
feebly for your death
in this alien place,
I wanted
so much to pick
you up, to hold you
like a baby,
somehow to make
up for those things
that had been absent
between us –
but I knew
I would not,
I could not,
intervene
in the present
our past had made.

It was the nurse
who finally took you
in her arms
and carried you
gingerly down the hall
to the treatment
room, while you
spoke almost

casually over her
shoulder, asking me
to please come
again.

Black Narrows

There are storm
warnings
from Hatteras to May
as the last
of the Chincoteague
tourists head west
over the causeway,
back to Baltimore
or Philadelphia
in the fickle light
of late September.
Suddenly, there are
no more summer
songs,
only this impatient
roaring gale
that keeps even
the gulls hunkered
down
and sends
whitecaps
across the broad bay
all the way to
Franklin City.

Snow

Here between
the Atlantic and
the Chesapeake
on a narrow finger
of land, snow
comes reluctantly,
if at all.

This is why,
when our
winter world
suddenly
turns white,
changing
everything
if just for a while,

it is as magical
as falling
in love for
the very first
time.

Backwater

I.
In the new century,
the sun still shines
on the backwater villages
of the Eastern Shore,
bleaching the bones
of the little wooden towns,
buckling the bottoms
of abandoned scows
flipped by the tides,
sending the long shadows
of barnacled pilings
across narrow creeks
at sundown.

II.
From Magotha
to Franklin City,
oyster houses are boarded
and locked, machinery
rusts, truncated
pieces of metal roofing
clang in the wind.
Stray cats
litter their kittens
in the jumble of
concrete and steel
that was once
prosperity.

III.
Ruddy faced waterman
still force a living
from reluctant waters
with brawn and wits,
still drink too much whiskey
and beer, still raise
hell down back roads
and in Norfolk honky tonks,
still nod to sleep
in their white boots
during raw weather.

IV.
Oyster and Clam,
Willis Wharf and Chesconessex,
Quinby and Saxis,
seaside and bayside,
the backwater moon
still floats out
from beyond the barrier islands,
charming the dreamers
in back bedrooms,
the quick-eyed daughters
with bodies still lean
and wild to the touch.

I Wonder What Sunsets Look Like In Istanbul

A face just covers a skull awhile;
stretch that skull cover and smile.
- Kerouac

It is a little thing
in the big and small
universal scheme of things,
the scheme that has
no beginning and no end
in sight, like a dusty, country
road in Accomack County,
Virginia which somehow
leads to Paris, Calcutta,
and the unrelenting moon.

My life, such as it is,
goes by like an electronic
whisper, like a silent
scream in a silent forest
beneath silent stars,
like wind finding
a crevice in a tottering
house to howl or moan
as it sees fit.

My life - always
more than it could
have been, always
less than it should have
been...

It went by
like a bus ride to Vegas,
like a drunken transvestite
on a bicycle to nowhere,
like a dog turd
bleached white
on a street in Albuquerque,
like a single red rose,
reaching into infinity.

My life went by like
Nietzsche and Kierkegaard,
like Heidegger and Merleau Ponty,
like that Dutch lens grinder, Spinoza,
while my buddies were laid
waste, without a clue, in
rice paddies and jungles
and were too dead
to wonder why.

And my life goes on
like a kiss that says
"maybe there will be
a tomorrow and maybe
there won't, maybe this
will be the last kiss
you'll ever have
so make it a good one..."

My life, one life among
so many in an incomprehensibly
teeming universe of life,
at fifty-four, feeling
the urgency to walk
barefoot in frost cold grass,
feeling the urgency to understand
the language of birds,
feeling the urgency
to love without remorse or fear,
feeling the urgency to know
even one thing really well,
feeling the urgency to answer,
once and for all,
one big question.

I Knew You Before I Even Met You

I.
It is late spring
in the first year
of our meeting.

It is dusk
becoming night

It is the first
cry of a whippoorwill
from some lost
world of time.

There is something
that passes
like a whisper
through
the dark wheat
at the edge
of the woods

into the middle
of my soul.

I am thinking
of you.

II.
The sad smiles
of tumbling houses
are covered
by honeysuckle.
The ghosts here
are old dreams
that inhabit the inner
spaces like wisps
of smoke
from 1932.

The cool
curved glass

of whiskey bottles
is scattered
like the bones
of dark-eyed
animals.

Why am I here?

III.
How many times
have you come
to me
in the guise
of dream?

How many times
have I listened
to the wind's
recriminations
without fear?

I realize
beyond all logic
that I need you.

When I step outside,
the stars begin
to fall
from the sky,
one by one,
like wounded
birds.

In Quinby

Life passes

like a quick wind
like shadows
over the marsh
like a hope
delicate as
dandelion spores
lifted beyond
the reach
of trees.

Life passes

as we turn
into driftwood
as we turn
into cordgrass
waiting
for something
nameless
at the water's
edge.

Life passes

as we walk
the fields of
early September
as we gather
plums at dusk
with our own
ancient hands

as we make love
in a room
lit by candles,
smelling of plums.

My Bones

Look around.

My bones are the ones
that glimmer cold blue
whiteness – scattered,
dislocated,

primeval,

like crab claws
strangled by sea weed
at the high tide line

or potstone
turned up in jagged pieces
by a farmer's plough.

General Motors chrome,
stag antlers, old
propane tanks rusting
into nothingness:

these too are my bones.

They are silent,
they have no voice.
The wind rises and falls
above them.

They sleep, awaiting
a forgotten incantation.

The Cabin

It was just
a squatter's cabin
on Metompkin Island.

I remember the green
hurricane shutters
on white clapboard
and the smell
of new, unfinished
wood when we
opened the door
for the first time.

I was nine years old
but it was like yesterday.

I remember the flicker
of kerosene lanterns,
sand in the cot,
the hushed whispers
of my parents behind
their plywood partition.
I remember long walks
along the ocean with
my grandmother
and the gifts of the sea:
whale bones and shark
carcasses, horseshoe crabs
and devil's pocket books
(but never a single gold doubloon).

I remember my
brother's red dump truck
in the white sand
and I remember
falling asleep
to the sound of the surf
and waking up
to the cry of gulls
and the smell
of bacon frying
in a cast iron pan.

I remember
nearly drowning
in the cove,
saved by my father
who I never knew
could run and
swim so fast.

And I remember
the storm
that took it all away
a few years later.
I remember
the final boat ride
out from Gargatha Landing.
We found our cabin
in the marsh
somewhere between
the island and the mainland
where it had been
tossed upside down
like a child's toy
and half-filled with mud,
green shutters
long gone.

The Heart Knows

Storm rage
or slow swell,
the heart knows
the flooding
of the tide.

And the heart
knows well
the ebbing
of the tide,
flotsam on the high
strand laid bare
beneath the
scudding sky.

The heart knows
the wind's sigh,
recriminations
whispered
in leaves seared dry
at the water's edge.

And the heart knows
the moon's cry,
the solitary weeping
of the moon
in the silence
of the sky

for the heart knows
there are times
the moon must
cry.

Plato

He was just a mutt,
the only one
in his litter
to survive hepatitis.

He was a survivor
but he was left
with the shakes.

"There's something
wrong with that dog!"
people would say.

Plato didn't care.
He liked to dance
and he would shake
in perfect rhythm
to rock and roll.

He liked Red,
White, and Blue beer
and The Grateful Dead
and he looked
especially cool
in sun glasses
and an old
sailor's hat.

He had a heart
as big as
Buddy Holly's Texas
and every bitch
in town.

Old shaky Plato...
when his time came
he just went into the woods
and never came
back out.

Glimpses

I.
The seaside night
licks its lips

and the marsh
gives up
its salty bones.

II.
Between the wing
and the shadows:

the owl's mask.

III.
Wind chimes
on the porch
of an old house
at the edge of rain,

spiders know
death comes
to us all.

IV.
In a pale light,
our faces
our hands
are maps
of back roads
we may never
take.

When All Has Been Taken From Me

When all has been
taken from me,
let me lie down
alone beneath
the stars.

When all has been
taken from me,
let me sleep
in silence
beneath the sea.

Do not wake me
to say the merciless
moon is seeking me
beneath the waves,
plaintively,

far into the deep.

Cold Rain

I
It is a cold rain
and I am missing you.
I ride just to ride
to places we have been
just to miss you more.

It is a cold rain
and out over
the marsh
the pine tumps
begin to blur
in the mist.

I feel myself blurring,
inner demarcations breaking down,
somehow liking this feeling right now.

It is a cold rain,
and here on the edge
of things unsaid,
a solitary pine
gnarled and disfigured
by many salt winds
stands like a sentinel
guarding the entrance
to some forbidden place.

And I wonder,
what is forbidden in this life?
Life is a continual rite of passage,
forbidding and yet forgiving,
a continual passing of sentinels.

It is a cold rain
falling on the
back roads leading
to back road places
where clapboard
houses are drawn into
themselves like
hushed whispers.

*Without you, I feel
like a hushed whisper,
I feel almost like a ghost
haunting these back roads
like a memory.*

II.
This could be
the future.
I think of you
in a warm house
with the rain
nothing but
a backdrop lullaby.
You are wearing
a cotton blouse
and faded jeans.
You are burning
incense and listening
to Etta James.
The light in your eyes
goes forth and meets
the coming night.
Your light wins.
It goes out into
the cold rain,
it winds down
the back roads,
finding me,
letting me know:
you are waiting for me.

About the Author

Kendall Bradley is a native of Accomack County on the Eastern Shore of Virginia and holds B.A. and M.A. degrees from the University of Virginia. Unlike most Shore natives and many of the "come heres," he does not hunt and fish but nonetheless can appreciate the enduring magic of this narrow spit of land felicitously wedged between the Atlantic Ocean and the Chesapeake Bay. Every now and then, he types a few lines on his laptop which sometimes, by a strange alchemy of sorts, are transformed into something that can loosely be termed "poetry." Kendall lives with his lovely wife, muse, and best friend, Ronda, in the small town of Melfa, a community which sprang up when the railroad came through in 1884 and which straddles the now abandoned track and Lankford Highway, a portion of U.S. Route 13 which, it is said, once ran from Maine to Florida and perhaps still does. *Backwater Musings* is his fifth book of poetry. Other books by the author include *Backwater Moon*, *A Butterfly with Teeth*, *Vicinity of Time*, and *At the Edge of Mercy*.

www.ingramcontent.com/pod-product-compliance
Lightning Source LLC
Chambersburg PA
CBHW070853050426
42453CB00012B/2179